In Praise of *On the Altar of Greece*

"The poetry of Donna J. Gelagotis Lee combines the sharp resourcefulness of the observer with the powers of the visionary. Her poems travel both in time and in memory to Greek villages and to Athens, bringing with them the spiky sensibility of a contemporary American woman. Never surrendering her complicated view of this complex world, she writes with vigor and a rapt, focused insight into the culture that spreads itself before her. Memory is a full-blooded character in her poetry, conjuring up each situation with a body-quickening pulse. With percussive rhythms and sensuous explanations, she draws us into her world, reminding us that she is at least two daughters of the titan Mnemosyne at once: Erato on the back of a motorcycle, Calliope in sunglasses languishing at the taverna." —Molly Peacock, author of *Cornucopia: New and Selected Poems*

"The poems of Donna J. Gelagotis Lee remind us that the word *poem* means "a made thing" in Greek, for the physicality of her poetry provokes the senses: "I feel my tongue / I taste the red mullet / and the octopus. I taste the sea / and the earth. I eat / the words." Like the hands she describes preparing food, Lee stirs up a rich linguistic concoction. And although she sometimes writes in the language of longing ("thirst / becomes the only word"), she is never solipsistic. Hers is a wisdom that acknowledges the self and its needs, seeing in them a commonality with the needs and desires of others. She knows that to empathize distinguishes the gifted poet from the merely good one, and enacts her compassion through the concreteness of her writing. With that physicality, she brings to life the numinous core of language." —Dean Kostos, author of *Last Supper of the Senses*

"Donna J. Gelagotis Lee's *On the Altar of Greece* actually does place its reader before, or on, an elevated place where the ceremony of everyday sublime life in Greece plays out. Without resorting to prefabricated classical references we've already heard to the nth, she includes us totally in everything she experiences and sharply senses there, the orange-turned yellow air, corners of walls, the shaded grove of stone men, the dark beach, a thread through looped thread, Poseidon cracking a wave, goat bells, "the speech unfolding / that flung dice against the white walls / until they wore eyes." Then, as important, there's the undertow of her subtle and deft suggestions of how the people in these scenes relate, and of the intriguingly close connection she herself has to them. Ms. Lee shows us a new, vivid, freshly layered world inside an ancient and long-known one. With her eyes, strong mind and solidly classical style of picturing in new terms this historical place turned myth turned "real" again, the journey of our time at this altar offers us a striking, immense set of views of a world we thought we knew, and still, wonderfully, do know in much richer ways by the end." —Don Berger, judge of the 2005 Gival Press Poetry Award, Poet Laureate of Takoma Park, Maryland, and author of *Quality Hill* and *The Cream-Filled Muse*

On the Altar
of Greece

by Donna J. Gelagotis Lee

Gival Press

Arlington, Virginia

Published by Gival Press, an imprint of Gival Press, LLC.

For information please write:
Gival Press, LLC, P. O. Box 3812, Arlington, VA 22203.
Website: *www.givalpress.com*
Email: givalpress@yahoo.com

First edition ISBN 1-928589-36-7 (ISBN 13: 978-1-928589-36-5)

Library of Congress Control Number: 2006934945

Photo of Donna J. Gelagotis Lee by Alicia Kozikowski of Pryde Bown Photographs.

Format and design by Ken Schellenberg.

For Dennis

Acknowledgments

Many thanks to my family, my friends, and especially my husband, Dennis, for his love, support, and years of patient critiquing and expert editing during the writing of this book.

Special thanks to Molly Peacock for her generous guidance and support.

My gratitude to Celia D. Jacobowitz and the late Judah L. Jacobowitz and to Jinny Baeckler and the Plainsboro Literary Group for their support and encouragement.

Thanks to Seva Hiras and Chrysoula Artemis for their assistance with the Greek language. I would also like to note the help of so many Greek-speaking people who were always willing to explain a Greek phrase or custom.

Grateful acknowledgement is made to Sweet Briar College, my alma mater, and especially to my many fine professors in the English and creative writing departments.

Thank you to Don Berger for choosing this manuscript.

Special recognition, with love, to my mother, Dolores J. Stark, a pioneer for women's rights in the workplace, for her love and her belief that a woman should choose her own destiny.

Thanks to the editors of the journals in which the following poems, sometimes in different versions, previously appeared.

"Hand to Hand" first appeared in *Asphodel*, Vol. II, No. 1, Fall 2003.

"The Cook's Wife" in *Atlantis: A Women's Studies Journal*, Vol. 28.2, Spring 2004.

"In a Vacuum of Night" and "The Meal" in *The Bitter Oleander*, Vol. 9, No. 1, 2003; Vol. 5, No. 2, 1999.

"The Seaside *Platía*" and "In My Mother-in-Law's Kitchen," originally published by *CALYX, A Journal of Art and Literature by Women*, Vol. 18:1, 1998; Vol. 20:2, Winter 2001/2002.

"History" in *The Cortland Review*, Issue 15, February 2001.

"Journey for the Bread" in *Crab Orchard Review*, Vol. 8, No. 2, Spring/Summer 2003.

"Visitor" in *Earth's Daughters*, Issue 66, 2005.

"Freedom," originally published in *Feminist Studies*, Vol. 29, No. 1, Spring 2003.

"Village at Noon" in *ForPoetry.com*, 2002.

"House," originally published in *Frontiers: A Journal of Women Studies,* Vol. 25, No. 2, 2004.

"Woman in *Áno Glyfáda*" in *Hurricane Alice: A Feminist Quarterly,* Vol. 13, No. 4, Summer 1999.

"*Ioánna,*" first published in *INKWELL,* Issue 13, Spring 2002.

"Afternoon in *Paleó Fáliron,*" first published in *Journal of International Women's Studies,* Vol. 4, No. 3, May 2003.

"Remembering You" in *Journal of New Jersey Poets,* Issue 39/40, 2003.

"Late Morning in *Áno Glyfáda*" in *Kelsey Review,* Vol. XI, Fall 1997.

"*Ioánna*" in *The Maine Scholar,* Vol. 16, Winter 2004.

"First Night in Athens" in *The Massachusetts Review,* Vol. XLV, No. 3, Autumn 2004.

"The Confusion of Time" and "Alone" in *The Midwest Quarterly,* Vol. XLIV, No. 1, Autumn 2002; Vol. XLV, No. 1, Autumn 2003.

"Confession" in *Phoebe: Journal of Gender & Cultural Critiques,* Vol. 17, No. 1, Spring 2005.

"Echoes of Battle" in *Rough Places Plain: Poems of the Mountains* (Salt Marsh Pottery Press), 2005.

"Exposé," first published in *the Seattle Review,* Vol. XXVII, No. 2, 2005.

"The Women" and "In the Sacrifice of Women"; "Your Wife" and "The Acropolis at Noon" in *Southern New Hampshire University Journal,* Vol. 20, No. 1, Spring 2003; Vol. 19, No. 1, Spring 2002.

"It would have been helpful to know" in *Terrain.org: A Journal of the Built & Natural Environments,* Issue No. 14, Winter/Spring 2004.

"At the *Laïkí,*" "Fish heads," and "In Utter Silence" in *WIND,* No. 88, 2002.

"The Fisherman" in *Wisconsin Review,* Vol. 35, Issue 1, 2000.

Contents

The Women

Into the circle of women
I entered, not knowing at first

the significance of their power
working as a double-pointed needle—

stitches, like deliberate words,
slipped into strong threads

in the small talk, gossip, and
debate, in the speech unfolding

that flung dice against the white walls
until they wore eyes

while winds lashed at the village square
with unruly tongues

and men wore the black
shadows of women unknowingly,

their deeds interwoven, their give-
and-take a bargaining that

surfaced even in the harshest
elements so that ultimately the women

wore this necklace of pride,
an adornment of rough rope,

frayed where it stretched and rubbed
against the corners of walls

they carefully walked around, which became
sinews of gold in the sunlight,

where their husbands escorted them,
beside their children, along the promenade,

their worth now displayed, portrayed
even to the other women who know

them silently, as they push the needle
through the last hours of afternoon,

as they hover
where the day does not move,

as they guide the thread along patterns
so neatly presented.

Arrival of the 6 a.m. Ferry

The Lésvian sun pulls in the
6 a.m. ferry with orange tongues, licks
of yellow. Light races
as I step onto the slab
of dock. Old Citroens and Renaults
carry the black silhouettes of couples,
sputter at the gate; fumes
choke up the entrance. Families
who have woken slowly, hours by bus
on the undulating coast, step
to the fallen plank, unburden themselves
with excitement in the orange light—the men
unshaven; the women broaden
with anticipation as they hold their arms
out to keep children
back. Cars hurl by me
from cavernous darkness into the orange
light. The port captain blows his whistle
hard, flaps his forearm down,
then up, and leans into the mouth
of the ferry. Behind him, passengers
wade into the fan of cars. Children
scurry in the parade. The scent of
cigarettes cuts into the orange air.
The sea cries its complaint, gulls
in for the ride. The line bottles
up, swells into automobiles,
overloaded produce trucks, gasoline
containers restoring their
balance. The captain
whistles, urges us
out of the way,
his body bending in emphasis.
The ferry tilts,
then regains its composure.
I reach the iron divider. Yellow
overtakes orange. Rows

of portside *kafenía, tavérnes,*
and souvenir shops
begin to bustle. Tiny cups of
Turkish coffee join tall glasses of ice
water, break day. Buses
pile up fumes. Bicyclists
pedal fast to beat
the noon heat.
The ferry rests
on a mirror sea,
like a body
listing.

Unremarkable moment,

slip your hand down my shirt
and feel my heart beat
so that I can measure your
insatiable appetite and
pace myself. I hear your
metronome
tap out its beat
as your hand touches my breast,
cool, like the hands of statues
poised in a museum park
on the Peloponnese,
where hardly an echo
reverberates, the artist's hands
now silenced on the broken
relics of an ancient age;
breeze, the reminder, drapes
the shaded grove of stone men,
stoic, phallic. Who would dance with
these headless men? If ancient stone
could come alive, what
would I feel here,
where women tended
the physical bodies of a nation,
washing its wounds, nurturing its young,
their hands moving over the skin
of politics while the words of men
chiseled into time?

Not Another Ordinary Day

The pots clang against
        the outdoor sink—the water runs.
It's morning—these are its sounds.
        Voices from the footpath. The sea breeze
carrying the donkey's bray and the farmer's call
        of the day's produce—
melitzánes, maroúlia, tomátes, lemónia.
        The milkmaid greets me
in the hallway—her wide girth takes up
        the space between me and my mother-in-law,
but *her* smile relates the news of a story—
        *eheis megálo mouní.**
I'm struck by the translation, thinking
        I misunderstand, but her face
reveals the truth. And I wonder,
        How does she know?
Her eyes never leave me and then
        she touches my arm,
as if to verify what she already knew,
        her familiarity almost violative,
but the ease of these women checks
        any ill feeling, and I brush it away, as I do
the hair on my face—a simple
        act, though the words remain.
And I begin to wonder how this woman
        who milks goats knows about vaginas—
I eye my husband with slight suspicion,
        then quickly erase the thought. The intimacy
of the women of the village has surprised me—
        they reveal their sex lives
as casually as they would
        a daily routine—and sex
often is, a neighbor explains, routine,
        obligatory. *Gámos,* as one young Greek man
told me, means *wedding,*
        and the slang word *gámo, to screw.*

Having children, the milkmaid explains,
>   makes a woman's life worthwhile.
Big teat, lots of milk; big vagina,
>   lots of babies? Nice to know I meet her approval,
as I am still childless—this justification
>   proffered, that I would have a good *mouní*.

* You have a big vagina (*mouní:* slang for vulva, vagina, female genitalia).

Visitor

With no rooms in town,
the ferry spitting out hundreds
of tourists, the local fishing boats
no longer cautious of the waves,
venturing into the wake
and far too close to ocean vessels,
a Greek woman took my passport
and led me up the mountain road.
At the top I was relieved
to see the entire village set
before me, as though it were a gift,
the sea deep blue, a lip of white houses
cresting its port, then at night lights
scattered about, the village bobbing
like a buoy, the little house on the hill,
where I was, still and quiet.

I paid for all three beds, so as not to be disturbed.
As I ventured into the village,
I found welcomes from shopkeepers, and children
trying to practice their English.
The warm *loukoumádes* melted on my tongue
as the sun intensified its beams
and shadows flew against the white walls.
The sounds of motorbikes
interfered with the late morning
struggling to come to a close.

And by evening, they reappeared, revving up
the night, near discos that pounded harder
than the sea on rock, that split the concrete foundation
of buildings so that the entire village shook.
I watched the motorbikes speed
down the road I had walked, heard the tourists
slip foreign words into the mountain air
that carried lavender and the still eardrum
of the night. I heard the tourists arrive
in the other rooms of the house, heard

the doors shut, and the stillness
return. And by morning when the rooster
called and the island air had recovered
and was stirred with the heat of an August sun,
I walked down the road into the village,
where Maria returned my passport
and I thanked her, in Greek, and stepped
into a small *tavérna*, my bag beside an outside
table, where a young Greek woman brought me
kafedákia, and I savored the strong bitter coffee,
rolled its grounds on my tongue at the bottom of the cup,
filling my veins with island blood.

The Confusion of Time

Watch the tree limbs waving
at evening when the night's moon
has hung itself in the last cloud
you see. What diffuse
light transforms your moment,
enters your skin, your blood,
until you dance in the moonlight
with the trees, without moving?
What limbs your arms make
as they stretch and climb
the night air, the air heavy
with moisture as the sea complains,
wave after wave! Village dogs
roam in packs, the scent of
a bitch in heat their trail
as the moon lies down
on the road, covered, bits
of light surfacing as though
a limb had appeared. The slow
night is like an empty lounge
chair I am tempted to lie in,
but the beach is dark and the waves
ferocious tongues. And I
smell only the distant pines
far on the mountain ridge, feel
the steep road and the breeze
suspending me. Here, I cannot
fall, as though time were a treetop
caught between heaven and earth.
Here, I am, like the untampered
island, breathing from my
diaphragm, no closed veins,
no strangled passages,
but this slow easy breath of air
circulating, falling, rising.

On Lésvos

Onto the foot
of Lésvian soil, an archangel
of the muse runs, pulling
the kite of dawn
through the port.

The cool bay of *Kalloní*
is in a salt frenzy,
mules tethered to wooden
poles, saddled with military
gear. Goats full with
milk, eyes
restless in the jiggle
of bells. On a ridge,
a thin road rises
into the inhale
of an ancient
island. Aeolus sends
a breeze off summer pine
as you and I coast
to the lowlands,
lean into
the turns.

Kalloní lounges
on a mountain rise.
Stípsi sends the cypress
into fields of honey.
Do we dare stop
to question old villagers
born before the Colonels
and the Communists,
who hauled shotguns to ferret
out men disrespectful
of women? Do you
and I dare go
into the clearing

to claim spring
water that finds its way
down the parched mountain?

At the tip of night, *Pétra*
will huddle. The church
of the sweet kiss will step
to the moon. But in summer
sun, it awaits
the sweat of men and
women struggling
to ask for help, sometimes
forgiveness. You step into
the butcher shop; carcasses
hang naked from a hook.
On the cobblestone path,
a priest halts, fish
in his bag, bread
under his arm. He
gazes down the moment
until my smile makes his
necessary. He hesitates,
keeps the blessed
ring hidden
in his furrowed robe—
no offer of food,
no drink,
only the sea breeze
wrapping folds
of his black cloth
against a stone
wall as the breeze gains
momentum
and makes its way
up the mountain
on a tail
of light.

Hand to Hand

You entrust them to me—
shelled walnuts in a bowl
half-full, then hand me
the mortar, while you
and your grandmother mix
the flour and sugar. I smash
them, pound them good and
when the deed is done escape
into the sea air that
curls around the corner
into the alleyway, where
you live. I step
away, feel the sea
before I ever see it, feel
its wet lips
and the caress of its wide
arms. I don't care
about the outcome
of the walnuts, pounded
into powder and flake,
I don't care how hot
the oven has to be or
what else is required.
I have succeeded
in what is expected
of a foreigner. I am
free. The air takes me
along the road like a hand
softly kneading
mine.

First Married

—Mólivos, Lésvos, Greece

Tourists gathered at disco tables,
the sea rocking itself
beside the mountain
onto which the dance floor
perched, as though we could fly.
Then the night hugged me
with its huge arms,
not really warm but large,
and I wondered if I should be
afraid, but wasn't until I looked up
at you, your large face
a moon, far away yet
beaming and pulling me toward it. Suddenly
I was rocking with the motion of night. I was
its partner, the mountains at my legs,
the sea air buoyant. It
was caressing my cheek, my legs,
my arms as your motorbike sped
along the coastal road.
There was nothing in the night
air but this place, which existed
nowhere, where I was.

Ritual in *Mólivos*

Cobblestone
underfoot, I
balance the steep
incline, breath
caught on the
inhale. At the corner,
the bakery door opens
to shadows of women
fingering eggs, loaves
of village bread standing
head-to-head. I scan
the room for
dark chocolate
buttressing
through flecks of
dough.

On the decline,
cobblestone slips
beneath me;
a parakeet's
green eye cages
the sea.
As my feet twist
to level ground,
the Aegean
sends a breeze to greet me.
I push the flaky
croissant up the waxed
paper. Chocolate oozes
onto my tongue, the
Lésvian sun
holding my face
in its hands, slipping
through the sheets
of phyllo
like air.

Along the Coast

—Athens, Greece

I couldn't smell the sea,
couldn't hear the waves
although they
shimmied in and the tide
came up over the rocks
and then retreated.
But I heard the boats
knocking against the dock.
I heard the water touching
their hulls and knew
your body wanted to feel
it instead of me.
I knew you wanted to be
carried out, wanted the moon
to tie you up at night,
its light bathing your body.
I knew you loved the
salty tongue of the sea,
the way you never trusted
her entirely. Perhaps that's why
the city took over
this body of water,
jets pulling their heavy bodies
through the air, hovering over you.
Perhaps that's why
I never knew
the sea was so close
and even looking out
could hardly believe how it
could touch so many
different bodies, so far
away, this sea
that was so distinct
from my memory.

The Fisherman

Yellow nets
rise like waves
before him.

The fisherman loops up
gaping holes torn
by the sea floor,
thrashed by fighting
fish. His eyes
list like the rope
of an anchor,
his fingers salt cut
and callused.
He stops
to finger
a cup of *kafedáki*,
its dark liquid
moving in streams
from porcelain;
he smiles
as he feels me
lift my camera,
his eyes gleaming
like jewel tide.

He shifts his weight,
then pulls the nets
toward him, skimming
the earth, in and out
of the shadows, his
thumb on the blistered
rope, pressing his life
into its frayed edges
with a healer's touch.

For a moment, he smooths
his face, lingers

on a thought away from
the nets, but just as quickly
they pull him back,
webbing their way over his legs
with weights
of wooden doughnuts spread out
like islands
on a yellow sea.
From burlap he pulls
the yellow nets, drapes them
from the wrought
iron of his front door,
and sits among streams
of yellow silk, sewing
as they wrap his life
around him.

The Seaside *Platía*

Mid-September.
Seats stare
wet and vacant
while village cats scramble
for what's left to eat
under the *tavérna* tables
the tourists have left.

Light bulbs strung
among creeping vines
along the wooden trellis
glare into the *platía*.

Inside the *tavérna*-turned-*kafenion*,
the one with the TV set,
village men linger,
taking in the smoke of cigarettes
with long, deliberate breaths,

their eyes fixed one moment
with political fever, the next
with the repetitious, checkered moves
at the roll of the dice.

Maybe it was the summer's
too-casual pace
or the cloudy licorice drink
they now sip,

letting their words slip
like gestures, a fling
of the cigarette tip,

salvaging some offhand remark
or slight offense
with sharp, contagious wit

that roars through the room,
sends them flung back
in the armless chairs, hands flying
in the air, smiles widening
into moon slivers,
eyes squinting through the shadows
of their heavy lids.

With a resounding slap on the back,
the thigh, they move into
one another's space.
Wrinkled men with mustaches,
smooth-faced men with
eyes as black and sharp as darts
fling their glances and grins
into the air
behind a wall of windows.

A black-clothed woman
stands at the edge
of the *platía,* watches
for a moment.

She knows
the men will not see her.

She remains in the shadows
as still as the fixtures.
Only the border
of her skirt lifts
on the sea breeze; strands
of hair that reveal themselves
from her kerchiefed head
blow away from her face.

Foíbi

Foíbi makes coffee
in a *bríki,*
gets the foam
just right.

As she tilts
the long handle,
rich liquid
slides off.
Muddy grains
sit like sludge.

Once women
poured their lives
from cups
turned
upside down.
When the black
residue
whirled its path
to the rim,
they read
the future's
splintered journey
as a fortune teller
would read
a palm.

Foíbi sets her brew
on a silver tray
with a hand-crocheted
doily, sugar white and
delicate, to cut its
mirrored gleam.

She lifts a tiny cup
beneath eyeshot,

a tale
delectably spun
on her lips,
a bite
of the offered sweet
on my tongue,
our laughter
spiralling
to the edge,
steam
floating away.

Mariánna Crocheting

Thread through looped
thread, the long needle
slowly intrusive. Women,
their eyes half-mast
moons, drop
village gossip, draw out
sweet aroma
from the hardest place, like
the lentils you simmered
all morning, until you
slide the embarrassing
secret from your mouth.

The needle jumps—a momentary
knee jerk—as the words
slip through
the eye to your lap,
down your skirt, run
in the dust. I cannot
stop them, your two sons
who want you to sign over
your house
with its new bathroom appendaged to the living
room and your long kitchen with its arrangement
of bent *bríkia* and dented pans. They tell you
the rooms will be let
to tourists. But you fear
that you will slip
into the walls
of a corner room
they reserve for you, the familiar voices
of your home muffled by the clamor
of constantly changing guests who
don't wish to know
your children or your husband or the house
before it had running

water or a toilet
inside. In the winter you
will feel the long-handled *bríki* but will not
know how it chipped under your thumb, how the
paint peeled off the edge
of the stove, how the chairs silenced themselves
in the snow of the season. You will pack
your doilies and scatter them
over the floor of your amnesic room
because you have
no furnishings to cover.

In the half-circle, nods.
Laughter
slices
like the bitterness
of a lemon.
Your hands hurry,
the mind crisscrosses.

One day you give me
a large rectangular doily
of a young woman lifting
a water jug,
as you have no daughters
            and no sons.

Theodóra

Six summers ago
you were a child,
pride of your father,
living in his eye.

Even now
his breath breathes
into you his life—
late nights and flashing
lights, jewels and pommeled
animal hides, the smell
of sweat on your skin.

That he should leave you
with a man like this
is your salvation,
a shadow to soothe you
when his call
sends shivers to your skin.

The square is empty now
and summer has let out
its tourists.
Leaves change in the shadows
of the eaves.
Black cats glare
at each passing face.

Do you remember?

Bearded men
bound shoulder to shoulder
dancing the *syrtáki*,
their song mixed
in the night air,
the women joining
by invitation.

He flung
the new money
with years of his sweat
and forgetting.
His moonless eyes swam
in the summer solstice,
the poverty of his youth
creeping up on him.

Ah! Do not remember!

Drink to new love,
to blood money,
the core of your
heart dancing
rhythmic, sensual—the pathos
of not-so-innocent men.

Your skirt will sweep
the dust from his seat.
You'll dance
into a slant of light.
Money will fall
through your fingers,
but he will press them gently
into a lover's hand—
fingers on the breath
of each summer night.

Your Wife

She stands in the street
and watches the sun
hover over a sea
of umbrellas.
She watches it shade
your face when you
tilt your forehead
toward her and down
as though you are looking
for something,
but it's only your hand
you have misplaced.
It is only a coin
in your pocket
that you have been
feeling, the smooth face
of someone you don't
know. She watches you
lean toward the sea,
hurl the colossal umbrella
with Herculean force
and then return
to your platform,
the haze of the sun your armor,
until you see her
and open your arms
and remember who she is.

Nights with the Olive Trees

They wrap their arms
around the stillness.
And we dance, without
touching, that silent
dance of memory,
bittersweet
on my tongue.
The overripened olive
between my fingertips,
my teeth.

I am the juice of it,
the liquid movement.
I am the one
you do not touch.
At the harp
the lips of Aeolus.
Along the length
of my arm,
the caress
of your hand
absent
as darkness stills
even the olive trees.

In the Sacrifice of Women

Your mother in black-flowing linens,
reminiscent of the robes of priests,
chops vegetables at the sink. Her body shifts
from side to side, her head covered
in the black kerchief of mourning.
Surely, someone has died, but died
long ago, because today, on this day
of wedding, only life, joining,
exalts. Even the diminishing
of whole eggplant and tomatoes and cucumber
yields a whole *mousaká, saláta,*
tzazíki. And the butchered lamb
simmers with mountain herbs, the sauce
of its bones and blood accepting the sacrificial
sheep. What part of yourself will you offer up?
Your brothers, returning from the fields,
a morning hunt for black birds, greet
one another, and you, and your mother, and finally
the guests. And we retreat to prepare
for the Spartan ceremony, to meet at the church in the village
down the street from the manicured park
of headless, armless statues dedicated to gods,
and heroes of the Peloponnesian War.
In cold November, when the mountains
unfurl winter, bare of harvest,
and mountain goats shimmy the crests
between here and Athens, in the breast
of the Peloponnese, *the heart of Greece*
the villagers say, you,
outside the church,
bury your head in the veil
of this day, your black eyes
shiny, reflective…
almost lifeless, like the endless
eyes of the black birds your younger
brother left on the kitchen windowsill
earlier this day, like an omen.

Readying for the Olive Harvest

To stand on the thickest branches
and knock the olives

out of the hold of summer
is to coax love

from a woman who has never known
how to be loved

without condition.
I have heard his is the hardest job—

trying to keep his balance,
limbs flailing in the air—

although the women submit for hours,
knees soiled with olives,

hands all knuckle in the cold.
A man stands above a field

of bent-over women, hurls
olives for them to handpick.

I have heard that each stick
is individual, a matter of pride.

But who will form the rod
to just the right shape?

And how does he know
when he has balanced it

to his height and weight,
to the grip of his hands?

Waiting

These women in black never
lie on the beach, like tourists,

seeking escape from time.
They never wait, watching the sea,

as the fishermen do at dusk,
casting lines into the murky water,

the ripe sky neither light
nor dark but merely a shot

in the eye of the monstrous future,
a stretch of summer, lying out....

If summer could be this beach,
might I return here, know

the sounds of the water
turning in on itself, the muffled

laughter on the sand, where bathers
flip over, their bodies

like long fish gleaming in the sun's rays
and moist with the spray of the Aegean?

The old women will always be
preparing, preparing,

their voices folding into waves.
When I look for summer in their eyes,

I cannot look deep enough,
although the surface may seem reflexive,

an innocuous buoyant body—
you will not touch bottom.

The Cook's Wife

The cook's wife
cleared tables,
straightened ash
trays, swashed
out glasses
with a wet rag
then dried
the dishes
with a cotton towel
she had ironed
the night before.

The cook's wife
met the fishermen
at the dock, bargained
for the best fish,
filled her apron
with fish smell
and the blood of fish
as she cleaned
and scaled them,
cut them into stew.

The cook's wife
handed plates
from the cook
to the waiters,
her arms strong
and wide, extensions
of the cook's
arms, of the cook
who wanted to take the food
to the tables himself.

The cook's wife
swept the floor
at night, cleaned

the tabletops.
The cook's wife
cleaned up
after everyone
was asleep.

The cook's wife
joined the cook
in bed. The cook's wife
was the cook's,
his heart beating
into the night
this steady
strong beating
to which she woke.

Free

Topless foreign women approached you,
asked for assistance, placed hot

coins into your palm, their fingers
sliding out of your hand,

as if taking more than they gave,
as the sea drew them out,

away from the beach and then
the sea met their bodies

and surrounded their bodies, wanted
to own their bodies as the tide

pushed and pulled on their bodies
and the water, so cool on their skin,

seemed giving, but the moon
tugged like a giant mouth

and you had to move with
the waves to escape the undercurrent

overpowering your body and when
it released you, when the sand

caressed your feet again and
sunset marked the death

of the day, your body appeared,
just like any other body

but scented with oil,
as if you were not at all

free.

Wild Rabbits

Your small boat... choppy
to the island of wild rabbits.

You dock between rocks,
lead me to clear pools,

small fish you spear
as I tentatively find footing

between stones at the edge
of the island—at dusk you again crank

the old engine—we never saw
wild rabbits you hunted winters,

cold in the breezy boat,
with the moon over the mountain—

your back to me now as you head
to port—the salt, your wide

body and fat tales enough
on this rough ride

back from the edge of an uninhabited island,
one huge rock, really, poking out

of the Aegean, one of many
small islands, where I could imagine

a rendezvous with the monsters
of our own myths, the ones

we never really see but that
remain even after we leave.

Afternoon in *Paleó Fáliron*

I determine the number of
blocks, decide to walk
to the *kafeníon* on the coast.
I know there I will have the option
of crossing the highway, putting
my face to the sea. If the gods
agree, I will feel a breeze
poised with salt and an eager-
ness to continue. But more than
likely, I will choose a table
on the corner of town, where
the policeman watches as if he
expects something to happen.
The offhandedness
of single women keeps him
alert—and newly married
women, like me, who
don't know the rules.

Poseidon cracks a wave
against the jetty so hard
I can hear it shatter like glass,
my tiny cup of Greek coffee calm
in the concrete village. Chairs
screech; the officer approaches
once again to ask why
I am here, where I live,
what time my husband usually
comes home.

Late Morning in *Áno Glyfáda*

Cucumbers pump themselves up
beneath the concrete
balcony while I pin
my clothes. The sun
does its job so well.

A neighbor lifts bricks,
smiles at me from
under the weight, as she does
often when we catch each
other in the work women do.

The Aegean wind picks
up my Greek husband's trouser legs,
flaps the corners of towels against
a rusting rail six lines
deep; I move the articles

farther from the building,
closer to her trellis.
She does not stop
to feel the midday sun
hard on her cheek
but passes
the pins by
her fingers so quickly
I do not see them. She
lets her empty basket
waver with a breeze,
then disappears

into a room in which
she rests her lips
onto the plump syllables
of afternoon.

After Siesta

The Athenian
on the neighboring balcony
juts his cigarette beyond the partition,
sees me as an
attraction
as he fingers his tiny cup
of Turkish coffee
with thick, rough hands.

My silver spoon clangs
in my cup, each circular motion
becoming more vigorous
and insistent, the rings
deepening
like church bells
that send the pigeons off
in a flutter and soon echo
in the city's hollow chambers.

He pulls his hand up
to smooth his mustache. Still
in the shadow of the concrete overhang,
I sip almost perfect foam. My lips
move in complete
silence, closing just enough to pull
the sweetness in, without letting him
know. How unsettling, the shared
vacancy. An ancient breeze
slides around us,
and we cannot escape
the rumblings in this awakening.

Ioánna

She cuts the bread
with the kitchen knife
she keeps on her bedside table

just in case—just in case
there is no bread;
just in case the Nazis come back.

She clings to it,
holds the bread to her chest,
hiding it with her round hands.

Still everyone knows.
We buy two loaves, one for us
and one for your grandmother

who stole scraps from the tables
of Nazi officers
to feed her five children.

"Could have been shot," you say
as she slowly lifts the loaf
from under the checkered cloth

in the kitchen at siesta, her footsteps
echoing down the hall, breath
and heartbeat.

Your mother once said, "*Ioánna,*
there's enough bread
for everyone." Still,

she carries each loaf
like something sacred,
slices the warm browned crust

into the flesh,
eats the white dough
of deliverance

just in case—just in case.

At the *Laïkí*

From my clothes-lined
balcony, I watch
the stalls go up—
iron to awning
to tabletop. Crates
line the pavement,
pile up on the
sidewalk, tomato
against grass, cucumber
buddies side by side, *maroúli,*
red beets, zucchini flowers.
I fill my pockets with change,
then round the corner, where Greek women
are returning, their two-wheeled vertical
carts bursting with greens,
transparent bags of
potatoes, eggs in cartons,
strung together, for
spanakópita,
mousaká
I have yet to make. At the edge
of wooden slabs
teetering on legs
of iron, I smooth
stalks of lettuce, shake
open a bag. The farmer's wife
eyes me, spits the price
in drachmas. The egg seller
narrows his brows as I check
each shell, then quickly slips
a handful of eggs
into a bag. I stop him,
Kathará, sé parakaló.
Kathará
einai, he retorts. And again
we bargain. A
stray dog brushes against my

leg, sweeps the ground
of scraps. I examine red beet
leaves I will boil
for a salad and garnish
with olive oil, the leaves hardly
recognizable with the aroma
of lemon. Orange-yellow zucchini
flowers lean toward me, but I resist,
their petals like lips. I hear
a farmer's wife arguing her
oranges are sweet as she pitches
blackened fruit into
a plastic bag, her customer
engrossed in contradiction.
Greek women push
their carts into my calves
just enough to bend the knee.
Their arms overreach mine,
their voices insistent in the
domain of food—the promise
of pleasure in the mouth.

By the Edge

I always preferred a table
right at the edge of the dock.

Looking down to the side, I
could watch the water waking

as fishing boats were going out to
or coming back from sea,

as if I could look down and find
the fish I could eat...

the sun just at its crescent,
the small caïques sputtering out,

as if to catch *it,* trailing
on the blood-red whip of its tail.

I ordered. The waiter
vanished. I didn't care to see

the fish on ice, eyes glazed over with
death. I didn't care to go inside.

Stray cats arrived, anticipating....
I'd fight them for it. I wouldn't give up

anything. They eyed me, let out their cries.
The waiter placed the fish before me.

My meal was that easy.
One cat rubbed against my leg

and then the leg of the table, as if
they were the same. The one-eyed cat

hissed for dinner, a place close
to the meal. I ate more quickly

than I wanted to—I ate without
savoring the sunset. The waters

darkened and the boats rocked
harder against the dock. I ate

until the bones showed and then
I left them on the table and

in a swoop the strays grabbed
mouthfuls, diving into the darkness

of the port, diving into the deeper
part of night, where I too

would ultimately remain, a scavenger
of circumstance.

Seized

You seized the hour by the tongue,
revealing your private moment so that now

it was one we shared, a force,
an intent scrambling with desire.

You lay still, you said, hardly feeling yourself,
much less him.

I was shocked by your confession
but not surprised at the act you described

so casually while shredding cucumber...
or were they carrots? You *did* pause,

your hands slack,
your eyes sinking in the sad fact.

Never had you felt
an orgasm, you explained, as though

revealing a recipe you knew by heart.
And now when the skin has begun to sag

with the weight of years of surrender,
when the body seems as though it has lost

the capacity to sanctify passion, you
offer up this confession to us, the women

of your life, as though we were gods,
as though we could change your mortal fate.

Hall

In our house was a hall
    like an artery
that throbbed with a pulse
    of the day's inhabitants,
an opening, where paths intersected,
    where we could begin
or end a journey, a thought or
    greeting, where we entered
into or exited, where
    we left guests we didn't care
to entertain, where food entered
    and laughter echoed like a bell,
where footsteps tapped out a heartbeat,
    where we let in or let out,
where we brought in or removed,
    where we pondered where we had been
or where we were going, like a map's abrupt
    route. Where the walls were larger
than the floors, as if an absolute rec-tangle,
    where the front door opened and closed
or stood ajar, a mouth open.
    The breastbone of the house.
A tiled runway.
    Middle finger of a hand.
Where dirt first arrived
    and last went. Where we had to
step into to step
    out of. What we traveled through.
What we left, like a remote island.

It would have been helpful to know

that winters on the island
seize the breath and hurl it
over the sea, which
sends it back again to lodge
in the throat. It would have
been helpful to understand
bitter autumn, its fruit laboring
on the tree, fat, black-
blue, the strange green of spring
still lingering. In the fields women
curl, down on their knees,
combing the earth for olives,
branches swaying overhead
from force, the arms of men,
the arms of trees, all strength
and heaving. It would have been
helpful to know summer's
undertow and the tenuousness
of the black sea urchin,
only its needles moving with the waves
but ready to release. While I ate,
iodine-red stained my fingers,
the caviar of the sea urchin
rolled on my tongue like clear
words, raw, antiseptic. I
scooped them out. It would have
been helpful to know
how to hold the probing
needles back, to keep them
from stinging.

Split

I lie down on the sand and the whole sky opens
up and gives me the troposphere to view, but it's too

sunny and the sun hurts my eyes, and the laughter of bathers
testing the water jolts me back to August on Lésvos

and the farmer, your neighbor, who's tying his donkey
to the chain link of the soccer field across the street

and picking oranges out of the basket to sell us
on the beach. His steps are so deliberate they brush

the sand aside and while he appears cautious he's
intent to sell, the cut orange juicy in his hand

showing its promise of quenching our thirst as he
exchanges fruit for coins and the change

jingles in his pocket as he trudges to the next blanket,
to the next bare bodies greased with suntan oil. He doesn't

care about nudity now, and we don't care how
dirty he looks because his smile is full light

and his eyes are clear and his donkey is waiting
patiently while tourist kids approach

to pat the animal's head, and it doesn't matter
that the sky is a perfect blue and that

if you look quickly you'll fail to notice
a division between the sea and sky, or that the olive

trees, rooted along the beach, never meant to root
here, where villagers rest on a wooden bench to cool

in their shade, and it doesn't matter if the figs
in the pan you carried to the beach were not washed

but freshly picked because when you bite into one
the seeds spill all over your tongue as if your tongue

had split open and you could taste a little bit
of the world and its divisive beginnings.

Fish heads

fill the sink
grey, rainbow
scales and eyes
glazed over with
death. The knife
on the edge
ready for my
mother-in-law's
grasp, the
quick slit
of the throat,
blood filling
the sink, on
her hands.
The water
begins to
run, streaming
over the gills,
the smooth skin
of hand, and tail.
I sit
at the edge of
the table
and disappear
as quietly
as the sunlight
that slides
through the
shutters
and over
the table,
that slices
a slant
of light
over the sink

so that
the fish
are steeped
in their own
misfortune,
so that
the water
has pearls
in it,
so that
I can see
her hand shiny
wet with the
deed, cats
crying
behind the concrete
wall, in the olive
grove, where they
will sleep—
the heads
are theirs.
I can hear
them clawing
at the wall, imagine
their huge scarred
eyes,
the thin, eaten
bodies awash
in her promise
of fulfilling
hunger.

First Night in Athens

Beneath the trellis, we eat
fried fish and potatoes.
Every bite is salty. The salt
sticks to my tongue. The salt
purifies my mind. My tongue is sticking
out in gesture, in plea.
It cannot retreat. I douse it with city water
but it does not budge. I have no
words to say until every Greek letter
begins to fall on my tongue. As I swallow,
the letters rearrange. When I open my mouth,
some words I do not immediately recognize
stumble out. And then slowly,
as the wine aged in oak barrels
slides down my gullet,
I feel my tongue,
I taste the red mullet
and the octopus. I taste the sea
and the earth. I eat
the words.

Journey for the Bread

As the olive trees interrupt
the sidewalk to send
shade along the street, I
greet the morning with almost
silent steps to the bakery.
The women in black pass me,
nodding a greeting
or glancing with a
partial smile, intent
on the duties of morning,
the chores of the day ahead.
In their hands, under
their arms, against their breasts,
the hot bread rests, bread
that will slip into
tzazíki, saláta, or the olive
oil of *fasólia*...
bread wrapped in gray paper,
uncut, crusty
village bread, *horiátiko*—I
have learned to ask for it,
as the villagers do,
by weight: *misó kiló, éna
kiló*—bread
that will be offered
by women, their faces thick
with folds, their eyes bright,
even fiery, as the day bursts
toward noon, when the food
for *mesiméri* will already be
in the oven or simmering on the stove.
Each woman will take
the loaf from under
the linen napkin and
slice thick pieces, leaving
the rest under the cloth,
within reach.

Chocolate Croissant

The baker's wife hands me
a warm croissant,
sokoláta, in a waxed
bag. I place it
on the front seat
of the silver Civic
and ride Mount
Hymettus. The houses
are startle-white; gardens
tend themselves in
the heat of an oasis.
At the base, the sea
is hand-stroked
into sky; a tanker, ferry,
yacht strike poses
in the haze.
Brush scurries
between rock. A flurry
of poppies hikes
into sunlight at the
rim of the cliff.
Each turn undulates
into unseen
routes as the
builder's stilts head
into the virgin air,
and a road I have
never taken spins
precariously
at the high
ridge. An old bakery
backs into rock
beside an Orthodox church
with rainbow streamers
in a small *platía.*
The street is dust
quiet. One stray dog

loiters at the flagpole.
The square stretches
asphalt
into lots
of wildflowers,
overheated with
bees. Behind me,
a bakery
door is an open
mouth.

Woman in *Áno Glyfáda*

Kerchiefed. Tendrils
of silver
touch her face;
she hauls firewood
on her back, lifts
bricks to fill
the shadows
at the base
of her whitewashed home.

Wooden clothespins
wedge my fingers.
Wind hurls sea spray
up the mountain. The sun
places it
on my cheek.

She hesitates,
breeze catching the grape vines
of the trellis, peaches
threatening to fall.
Her eyes
quickly
keep their silence
and traverse the boughs
of her tree
where its pears ripen
over
my balcony.
Doulía, doulía.
*Ti na kánoume?**

Her lips reach back
into a smile,
the weight
of a fallen axe
on the words

I no longer need
to translate.

*Work, work. / What can we do?

Turncoat Sea

In that boat knocking
as the tide rolls in:

a lost soul—an empty vessel
within a larger one, one of immense

depth and expanse, of force.
That's why I stand somewhat

silent, my lips half-pursed as though
a sound could escape, as though

the wind were my own, the breeze
something I could muster. The boat

lulls, then with an unseen surge
that swells beneath it it lurches

toward land, as though it *wanted*
land but was anchored,

tied to the sea and its own eternity,
like a wishbone of water

no one could separate for luck
or salvation.

This vessel no one would board
tonight aches in the harbor,

moored, with a long line to the anchor.
I don't want to dive to reach it—

I don't even want to get wet.
I'm content to join in with

the turncoat sea, which will leave
again the land it came to please.

Confession

The elliptical porch
surrenders to a flowering
jasmine tree, its
tender branches partly
portico. A half
moon sends blue
light over the leaves
as they tap out subtle
songs in the summer
air. You, too,
are newly married. I
met your mother on
Crete. Your father
proudly showed me his lemon
trees; your younger
brother slung black
birds he had shot—slivers of
dark in their death eyes—
over his shoulder
the way I used to hang
a pair of skates.

Your husband, from Athens,
gets up to join mine
in the kitchen. You
lower your head
in the cross
of light and whisper
that he has hit
you, because
it is his duty
and because
a man needs to
hit his wife
once in a while.
You become quiet
as he returns, and
lean back

into your place;
the heavy moon
weighs
into the chair,
spinning you
on the mosaic tiles
like a Delian sacrifice.

Gone Swimming

Who could blame the baker,
who wore the flour

of wheat, who coaxed life
into dough with precise hands?

Who could deny those hands
the mystery of water

as it molds the sand, the land,
as it slips into flips

then the minute particles
that bind us finally

to the earth? The sun and the wind
had made up in *filia*

and the beach reflected
every perfect summer onto a powder

sky. Had Aeolus set
the course this day?

On the bakery shop door,
a note, scribbled off quickly,

tacked with the wind.

Alone

The blood slows and time itself
lies back, holding the sun, resisting
its weight, shadows slicing off pieces
of the afternoon. And then my eyelids fall
and I drift into summer sleep. A slight breeze slinks
around the corner. Flies stick to the window.
The silence of afternoon is complete.
And now time meditates on the cool balcony.
When I wake, I touch time's hand.
I have stepped into the house of evening.
I watch the sun set and think a slice of day has fallen.
The heat disappears. The pulse of night throbs
in my veins, just beneath my skin.
It is my own heat that I feel now.
It is my own heartbeat that pushes me through time,
that beats in the night's visible neck.
How vulnerable I will be on this road by the lashing waves,
where village dogs roam beneath the flesh moon.
And in the voiceless chatter of the cicadas, vibrating
on the wind—the thick tongue of the sea, your lost voice.

Echoes of Battle

Along the mountain road a goat herder
stops while his flock grazes
the greenery on this route from Athens
into the heart of the Peloponnese.
Today the clouds skim the gray from the sky,
seem to settle over the road ahead that dips
into fertile valley, where armies of men rose
up on their way to Athens. And
the women in black no longer remember
for whom they mourn, their faces
like paths in the dark,
their eyes hollow to hell with
fatigue. In the eye of the moon
a confused sun bursts. In the heat
a troubled landscape. Goat
bells ring out over the ridge. I
can still hear a faint resonance.
As I approach, the young goats tremble,
searching for bits of green
on a mountain range blooming
out of the bloody earth.

Athens in August

I swear
they are babies' cries.

But then the paw
claws into the moon-slit
pupil; I am assured
this is animal.

The long, hollow cry
beyond alley cat
splits the central darkness
of the city
so that I too
can feel the
touch of deep
desire—primal,
its first hurtful
thump,
then pitch-high
         scream.

Walls of concrete enclose,
rise until they suck in
my breath.
The sky
in relief.
Its light a mere reflection
of the city.

In the middle of my bed
I sink
into outline,
and the room breathes
for me.

Escape to the Night Air

So simple, your eyes, like purple martins taking flight.
So simple, the flutter of fingers on my wrist,
like tiny pulses, the beating of wings elementary.

I threw the sun over my shoulder, and fled, counting every step
on every stone with the muscles of my body, my nerves
like gears of a clock rolling minutes along.

The streets left a film of my journey,
spots on a negative,
the torture of moments wound too tight.

Not a human shadow on this path besides my own.
The buildings shuttered and the continuous call of the cicadas
demanding an answer.

A piece of myself will remain on this road, where tourists
    and villagers
walk to and from the square, the beach, the next village
and at night, beside the sea, the branches of the olive trees
    beg for company.

The island will soon be dark, devoid of words but full of voices,
and stray dogs will scamper along the road to follow the
    scent of heat.
It seems no connections will be made—just a long searching,
    a tremulous trill of insects.

But the night air will linger on the limbs of olive trees.
I'll find it on my arm, heavier than the weight of my own limb
hanging, still, even as I lengthen my stride.

The Acropolis at Noon

If I am quiet, I will hear Socrates
mouthing beyond the columns
of the Parthenon, his pupils
on the steps beside me,
their tongues protruding, while syllables
drop there. A scramble ensues
to order them, so that the sounds
align and meaning falls logically
down the throat. I am looking hard.
The noon sun is baking me into stone.
I understand how the elderly bend over,
their faces shielded, their own shadows
like brims of hats. What are they thinking?
What juice has dripped off the tongues
of the learned? The steps are dry.
And tourists line up at the gate.
The concrete spreads itself under the sun
beating and beating into the pores,
parching the throat, so that thirst
becomes the only word.

Athens at Dusk

Summer drags its net again
as the mountains let breezes
dock at sea, as if waiting for permission

to enter. Here, on a mountain high
in *Áno Voúla,* I watch you sizzle
the clouds you smoke, fading

into what the sun has left.
I almost welcome night—so brutally
open, and feigning nothing,

cool, distant, yet enveloping,
with indifference I could
sink into, as though to lose

myself with no answers
and, finally, no expectations.
Wisdom, a few words

and mostly unanswered questions.
So I ask a question of the city—
why do we wait?

We have all waited.
We still wait.
Hundreds, thousands of years….

Night stretches out
and swipes stars from the sky,
and the moon almost disappears.

Cafeteria on Syntagma Square

The *kamáki* in the cafeteria
believes he has spotted

a tourist who will succumb
to his quick grin and cool talk

but I turn his spear
around with a glance

and with force it hits him
as I snap out *no*

in Greek and proceed to the
cleanest bathroom in town

where all the tourists would go
if they knew.

To the Olive

Bitter olive,
what fields are these
that lay grip to the earth,
that spread roots and
entangle years into the trunks
of your trees? What limbs rise up
from this sprouting? Strange olive,
fruit of fall, oil
of anointment, of digestion,
of the lamps that once
lit the night, what unique history
stores itself in your belly?
The smell of brine as it cures you
ascends my senses. Now, the smooth
shine is final in its own oil.
Your persistence produces
abundance, keeps you
so long on the autumn tree,
plumping in the sun, its rays
probing you.

House

I reached through the bars
to my homeland but all
I touched were your
clothes hanging on the lines,
the words of my new language.
In this house was the housewife's
poetry. In the chores,
the endless tasks to maintain
order within, to maintain order without.
But the house never spoke to me.
It kept its music to itself.
It was a house of crosscurrents.
If the windows opened, each
door slammed, and anything with words
written on it would fly
into the air, into another space.

English Teacher

A secret wish she coveted
      left her open to ridicule,
her future their past, decision
      hard as the chores she completed
each day with the hand of Jehovah
      on her shoulder, the taste
of servitude clinging to her sweat.
      It wasn't known yet
that choice was hers, but some hint
      of it swung down like a serpent
from a branch. She studied
      what was now laid out before her.
She felt foreign letters on her tongue.
      She heard their souls and desired
them. Soon she'd put them in the wash water.
      Soon she'd hang them out to dry.
Soon she'd kneel beneath a man
      pleased with her obedience, as
the other women would not free her,
      who would not free themselves,
their fear stronger than faith.
      Which words would be erased?

Neighbors, *Paleó Fáliron*

On the ledge
in the living room
votive candles
lit for her dead
relatives, her face
half a glow, the
other side a
shadow that
leans into
the hallway.
Her husband
never completely
enters
but stands back
as if to catch
her. She moves
slowly like
afternoon light
while pictures of
children announce
her life.
A soft breeze
drifts around
corners,
into the kitchen,
and out the door.
The rustle
of leaves, smell
of geraniums,
the aroma of
coffee past
boiling. She
watches us,
her eyes
large and tender,
not knowing
if we will
last.

Exposé

Three neighbors in black pass by.
I never met their husbands.

Today their white faces seem whiter,
as if the light in shadow,

as though the sun were always behind them
or their faces were always downcast,

making another, different shadow on the ground.
They each greet me as I sweep the steps,

stepping down one by one until I too
reach the street, a dirt path,

once only a footpath between houses.
Years stretch out between us.

Time, a footbridge I cannot pass
over. And the women study me

and perhaps wonder why *I*
sweep the soil away,

I who have lost no one, who
have borne no one, who seem like

a tourist with my foreign tongue,
I who wear my hair full and uncovered,

who bare my arms and my legs
to the sun, who will finish

my chores with this task only,
I who will expose myself

to a cloudless sky.

The *Kamáki*'s Ashtray

She couldn't wash your ashtray
full of cigarette butts,
couldn't empty the bits of paper,
charred edges of tobacco
rolled by hand.
She couldn't.
She let the sun rot them,
let them dry, as though they could
ignite all by themselves
and some part of your soul would burn
as it does at the end
of each cigarette that forms
a part of your mouth, in and out,
like the foul language that interrupts
the smoke, the rings you mouth
with the lips that circle a hundred
women's mouths each summer.
She couldn't touch them, wouldn't move them,
and each day you simply added
another and another at evening's
foot and when the night laid
its grip on the city and
everything that lay between it
and its past, including you,
as though you were a bridge
to old habits, ideas
about women that suited
you, puffed you up
even without the smoke,
let your hands form fists
in front of their faces
after making love like a gentle
man. Rules. You play by the
rules you like and let your
force fling itself haphazardly,
as you do a cigarette butt... *but:*
that small word that serves
to justify each deed.

To the Female Octopus

On the line you hang, stunning octopus.
More like the drying gelatin of future food
than the smart female who nearly starved,
protecting your thousands of unborn beneath
the water in dark canopies devoid of entrance
or exit. Clever octopus, mistress of disguise,
deaf but keen of eye, you could not have heard
your own cry when the diver's spear struck and afterwards,
on a hot beach, your body slammed till death
on the smooth stone of captivity. Is there not a tear
left drying in your eye? At you, I cannot look,
as you remind me of my own misfortune.
I cannot even think of how sweet
you could taste, of how the many arms you used to reach
into the crevices of your liquid air will feel on the tongue.
Let me think, instead, of those who escaped,
who dove away when the shiny object plunged toward them.
Let me marvel at their cunning, deciphering
the turns and dips around them, their agile bodies
moving freely through the water.

In Utter Silence

I have watched your mother
at the sink, scrubbing, peeling,
rinsing, laughing, crying
all hours of the day,
for someone was always hungry
or thirsty and the dishes and the
food presented
a continual stream of activity
calling her. The light played
at the window opposite her,
on the clothes that hung above
the concrete patio,
or settled into the field splattered
with olive trees and stray cats
waiting for scraps she would
fling off the plate
with hardball force.
I never walked directly
in her path, my steps being
too hesitant, too angular and
deliberate, too self-conscious.
Time splayed its fingers across
the table for me, and I locked
mine into them. I looked
into every day as though it were
the vacation of my middle age.
She had no fantasies
about time and life, but death
held a promise I would never
understand. Death for her was a path
to rebirth, the life of the spirit
as life on earth in constant
joy, the joy she had trained
herself to believe in every day
as she left and returned to the kitchen sink,
water running over her hands
and down the drain

like the life force
of her, desiring
nothing for
herself alone,
as though to desire she would
have had to step away from
that sink long enough
and let that space seal
itself with utter silence, not a breath
hushed, not a word
swallowed into oblivion.

Too Far

On your motorbike, I never feared
the climb, the twists up mountain
roads, and the long coast down; no

matter what the terrain, we
would prevail, as if a god
were watching us, counting

the turns. Salt beds stretched
out to the bay—
the flat road crossed a one-lane

bridge we rode around
with the solitary ringing of a goat bell,
a donkey's bray, and the wind

steadying gulls and swallows
that swung over the cove
while we approached mountains

again—limestone rock, sharp
turns with icon boxes to the dead—
the stones shot out by our motorbike

tumbled unimpeded from guardless cliffs.
And when we arrived at the spring,
near a lookout among the olive trees,

the sea gleamed before a church that rose
into the sky, a tribute to those lost
to find their way.

What would save us? The day
was as pure as water springing up,
the air crisp, the sun settling

onto the village like a blessing;
even the waves dazzled us,
even the olive trees shined silver.

Even when the winds picked up
sand, when the sea went wild,
we stayed, as if we might miss

one moment of our salvation.

In a Vacuum of Night

On a mountain street stray dogs
roam in a pack, humping a bitch in heat,
stuck in the hole of night,
where moonlight only skims
the surface. The desperate wind
begins to roll down the mountain,
dragging my scent along, and now
mongrel dogs gather from miles around.
They creep under the carport.
They scour my garden
then gaze up at my balcony.
Their eyes cut through the sliding glass.
Their whimpers drip blood
from the branches of the peach
trees. When I bark at them
to leave, my voice appears as a howl
and leaps out of my skin
into the night to catch
a breeze and fly toward the sea.
The dogs disappear. The wind dies.
I stretch out in a hammock of dream
between my house and the sea
and sway effortlessly, wind
my own indecision,
keeping me suspended
in a vacuum of night.

The Meal

Evening joined us
at the table, the
two wooden chairs
askew, the shutters
open, window framing
the bare night
like this empty
room still and quiet
and telling me that
the season has its
own intentions.

So I waited
for the cool
cucumber salad,
for the fried
potatoes, the oiled
tomatoes cut into
quarters, lettuce
crisp like the sea
breeze on a tangential
corner.

The room
was like art, the
wood used for more
than what was intended,
wooden chairs webbed
at the seat, slits
in their backs,
the clothed
tabletops clean,
our ashtray askew,
the cook sweating
over the grill
behind the glass
cases of fish
as he made us

the meal and we
dissolved onto the room's
tongue, unaware of the fingers
of our surroundings
lifting us into the mouth
of this slow
evening.

Village at Noon

I look at the sun by mistake
and it rolls like a fireball
down the street, a burst
of yellow. The street has been
wiped clean, and no one
walks except me. Onto
its tongue I step and it pulls me
into the square
where men are stunned
on *tavérna* chairs, their cigarettes
charred, their stubbled faces
red with the noon heat.
When I reach the uvula,
I peer into their throats,
into the throat of the entire village.
I smell the stale cigarettes,
step aside the coffee stains,
cough on ouzo fumes.
I hear their stark remarks
as the larynx rumbles.
I want to know what lies
in the stomach of a village
but dare not leap,
nor do I slow my pace
because the entrance
is disappearing
and I need to turn
to find a way out.

Freedom

She ironed her anger
into his clothes at 2:00 a.m.
while his mother slept
in the spare bedroom
and he was upstairs, unaware.

She ironed shirt after shirt,
trouser after trouser leg,
towels and sheets. She ironed his
expectation, and hers, into
the *rouha*,* feeling the doing of it
was a brouhaha of sorts, as
the Greek rolled around her tongue
like a washing machine. The humor
rose into her skin, leapt into
her hand and fingertips and
she felt she could iron everything
happily in that insane
state, as the clock
dropped the night seconds
into a glass of water
and she heard them dripping,
then poured them into the iron
until her mother-in-
law appeared, her face
a round moon in the doorway,
her frame a bush—
when she opened her mouth,
she began to burn, flames shooting
out words—*Ti káneis tóso argá?***—
that lashed
a question with a judgment
at its end, a disappointed,
albeit pious,
gaze, as though she were

sent by God to bring
a message of temperance.

*clothes
**What are you doing so late?

French Fries and *Tzazíki*

Every night, it was French fries and *tzazíki*
at the upstairs *tavérna* over the *platía*

by the sea. The owner was cook
and knew us. His salad was fresh,

his fried potatoes crisp, and the *tzazíki*
creamy and cool with the subtlest bit of garlic

coming through. I wanted nothing else—
no words, no fish, no meat, no bread.

The night was a perfect balance.
The dark huddling in among us.

What was there to say?
The tongue was engaged

and wanted nothing to do
with speech—it wanted

what I wanted—taste
and salivation.

The Cove

I stand at the edge of the cliff,
perched on the wind, the sun beating,
repeating, "I will let you feel your
pores, water seep from your
skin. I will bathe you on rocks,
or I will bake you into this
furious landscape." A mountain breeze
rushes the smell of winter pine
through the olive trees,
their huge fruit burgeoning
on the limb. I feel the weight
of a man's determination, my
arms tremulous. Tentatively, I
slip one foot into the crevice
of ancient Greece but stop, lean
into the anchor of the other.
I have done this before
with you. A lizard
strays between rocks—the
only rustle, a few
strands of burnt grass
in the blue-balled
stillness. My silver Civic
opens its door to a foreign country.
The breath of the sea persists
as I wheel
to smooth surface,
the Aegean rippling at arm's
length, now simply
a landscape.

In My Mother-in-Law's Kitchen

Her Bible flung itself open
on the kitchen table
beside wide-mouthed bowls
and jagged knives. She sliced
open the squash, spooned out
the seeds, and cut the pulp into
that mouth of a bowl, then
smashed the juicy pulp, adding rice and
cinnamon and sugar. Such a blend
of sweetness and vegetable, something
that reminded me of pumpkin,
the hollowed-out face we lit
with candles, whose seeds we discarded.
The strange mix of delight and mystery
like hauntings of light and dark. I watched her
roll out the phyllo, never ripping
the paper-thin sheets as she
layered the gleaming orange mix
sheet upon sheet upon mixture.
Her heavy arms swung
and lifted and lowered,
strengthening in the labor
of this sacrifice, of duty to family
and to God, who commanded duty.
She glowed with each completed chore
as though she had given it up
instead of herself. I saw the glint
of flame in the pupil, the
eye of the soul widening
and then closing as the light within her
grew and gleamed incessantly.
I had to leave. I started
to burn inside. It was my self
begging for forgiveness for sins
I didn't know I was committing.

I saw my self taking
the knife and cutting the squares
of the *kolokithópita,* making
tiny cuts for air holes in the dough,
and so pleased. I saw my self
attached to the apron, strung
to the sink, a long ball-and-chain
between the front and back doors
with enough length to sweep the
porches, to fling the donkey droppings
from the street into the flower pots,
and to bend over with a short broom,
sweeping the loose dirt off the firm dirt,
keeping the dirt out of the house,
where I would live. I saw my self
and ran without speaking any language,
without running, except inside,
until I finally packed my
belongings in tight, padding the
clothes down so I could fit
every last item in and
leaving with a smile
that country that had
been my escape.

One Road

One road cut through
the village. One road
to your house. One road
on foot, by car,
on horseback or mule.

Along this road you may find
my exhale, when mornings
the breeze filled my body
and traveled through my
blood. Now I am filled
with the oxygen of an
island, where the sea
never forgets its responsibility
or force. From your balcony,
my eyes traveled down the road
and deepened a hue and now
I believe my pupil is a permanent
dilation, even though at the time
I'm sure it constricted to a point.

The breeze curled along the edges
of the railing and enticed me.
And I can still feel its hand
on my arm, leading me
on a journey from which I could return,
leading me to take a next step.

And I leave you to determine
what cells will divide
in the sunlight, what part of you
will photosynthesize. Forgive me.
I am riding on night's tail.
I have forgotten the side streets
of our previous life.
I am walking to the village

and back. I am walking out of town.
I am walking to where the road
curves beyond the dock,
where the sea slaps the boats
into submission.
I am feeling the water on my feet
although I remain
on dry land. Dusk,
what plans do you have
for me?

Misconstrued

In the darkness I gather the winds
while Aeolus sleeps and on the cusp of
moon I fashion my own boat to
light my path across the sea. I'll
be sure of my return and will not
be lured by islands of sirens or dumb
beasts. I'll summon gods before me

and they'll drink my words with their wine;
they'll summon earth itself to turn my
mortal journey to suit *me,* instead of fate,
for I have their own whims at my disposal
and it is not for passing beauty
that Zeus tosses back the golden apple,
but the womb of maternity guided

to encompass even the gods like a cradle
in an ocean, which could hold them,
feed them, embrace them. Really
they'll soon ask so little, their own fantasies
becoming easy to fulfill. Connecting land to land,
water the buoyant womb of the earth,
I'll cross the seas for my own gift.

How wicked I've become, I'm afraid,
tending to myself like a feigned goddess,
like Demeter before the harvest or
Aphrodite basking in garland,
anointed by her own olive branch. See
how I command myself and therefore
others. You'll dare neither wrath nor passion,
for each can be misconstrued.

Remembering You

Gamma, epsilon....
Slowly your name spells itself
to me, my tongue catching the letters
along the contours, bulging through
interior openings that flip the letters
onto their backs. And I have
forgotten what they said to me.
I have forgotten the taste of your alphabet.

History

—*Pétra, Lésvos, Greece*

Just remember
the coast
as it is in
September, summer's
back at its heels,
the olive trees hanging
fruit that plumps
dark into the night,
the half-deserted
street a chilled
artery, blood
slowed. I know
the moon has no
friends at this time
of year and the men
will go out to
the olive trees to knock
the plumping fruit
out of the trees,
onto the netted
ground, where women
curl into cocoons,
their fingers unseen
as they blacken
with fruit, their curved
backs bending into
the landscape.

I can see the men
on the edge
of this summer after-
noon, picking out
sticks to be carved,
getting the feel of
the *débla,* already

testing its weight and
contemplating
balance in the limbs
of the olive trees,
in the limbs
of women who will crisscross
the hard ground,
women who will scavenge
for olives, their knuckles
blossoming black, their fingertips
dug into earth, the raw
afternoon bearing down
until each shaft of
light disappears and
dusk is more than
a memory of passing
with its heavy hand
and its delicate fingertips
brushing the fields,
lightly touching
all the landscape,
the trunks, the
leaves, the trees,
until night arrives
with promises
for tomorrow.
I can see each woman
with night already
on her face, the mountain
underfoot, as she heads
home while the men
join each other at
the *tavérna* and lick
ouzo from the rims
of short glasses.

Glossary

bríki (plural: *bríkia*): small pot with a wide bottom, a long handle, a narrow neck, and a lip; used for making Greek-style coffee

débla: stick used to knock olives off the branches during the olive harvest

fasólia: legumes

filía: friendship

kafedáki (plural: *kafedákia*): diminutive for a cup of coffee

Kalloní: town on the island of Lésvos

kamáki: harpoon; also refers to a man skilled in the sexual pursuit of foreign women

kathará: clean

kathará einai: they are clean

kolokithópita: pumpkin/zucchini pie made with phyllo

loukoumádes: honey puffs; small doughnuts deep-fried, coated with honey, sprinkled with cinnamon, and sometimes sesame seeds, and served hot

maroúli (plural: *maroúlia*): lettuce

melitzánes: eggplants

mesiméri: midday (typically between 2 p.m. to 3 p.m.)

Pétra: village on the northern coast of Lésvos

platía: village, or town, square

sé parakaló: if you please

sokoláta: chocolate

Stípsi: village in the mountains of the island of Lésvos

syrtáki: popular Greek folk dance that begins with a slow
    tempo and speeds up; performed in a line or a circle

tzazíki (also *tzatzíki*): sauce or dip made of yoghurt,
cucumber, and garlic

Books Available from Gival Press

A Change of Heart by David Garrett Izzo
1st edition, ISBN 1-928589-18-9, (ISBN 13: 978-1-928589-18-1), $20.00

A historical novel about Aldous Huxley and his circle "astonishingly alive and accurate."
— Roger Lathbury, George Mason University

An Interdisciplinary Introduction to Women's Studies Edited by Brianne Friel & Robert L. Giron
1st edition, ISBN 1-928589-29-4, (ISBN 13: 978-1-928589-29-7), $25.00

Winner of the 2005 DIY Book Festival Award for Compilations/ Anthologies.
A succinct collection of articles written for the college student of women's studies, covering a variety of disciplines from politics to philosophy.

Bones Washed With Wine: Flint Shards from Sussex and Bliss by Jeff Mann
1st edition, ISBN 1-928589-14-6, (ISBN 13: 978-1-928589-14-3), $15.00

A special collection of lyric intensity, including the 1999 Gival Press Poetry Award winning collection. Jeff Mann is "a poet to treasure both for the wealth of his language and the generosity of his spirit."— Edward Falco, author of *Acid*

Boys, Lost & Found: Stories by Charles Casillo
1st edition, ISBN 1-928589-33-2, (ISBN 13: 978-1-928589-33-4), $20.00

Casillo's boys are hustlers, writers, models, cruisers, lovers— complicated, smart, cool, witty, lusty, and romantic. "...fascinating, often funny... a safari through the perils and joys of gay life." —Edward Field

Canciones para sola cuerda / Songs for a Single String by Jesús Gardea; English translation by Robert L. Giron
1st edition, ISBN 1-928589-09-X, (ISBN 13: 978-1-928589-09-9), $15.00

Finalist for the 2003 Violet Crown Book Award for Literary Prose & Poetry.
A moving collection of love poems, with echoes of Neruda *à la Mexicana* as Gardea writes about the primeval quest for the perfect woman. "The free verse...evokes the quality and forms of *cante hondo*, emphasizing the emotional interplay of human voice and guitar."— Elizabeth Huergo, Montgomery College

Dead Time / Tiempo muerto by Carlos Rubio

1st edition, ISBN 1-928589-17-0, (ISBN 13: 978-1-928589-17-4), $21.00

Winner of the 2003 Silver Award for Translation—ForeWord Magazine's Book of the Year.
This bilingual (English/Spanish) novel is "an unusual tale of love, hate, passion and revenge." — Karen Sealy, author of *The Eighth House*

Dervish by Gerard Wozek

1st edition, ISBN 1-928589-11-1, (ISBN 13: 978-1-928589-11-2), $15.00

Winner of the 2000 Gival Press Poetry Award.
This rich whirl of the dervish traverses a grand expanse from bars to crazy dreams to fruition of desire. "By Jove, these poems shimmer."— Gerry Gomez Pearlberg, author of *Mr. Bluebird*

Dreams and Other Ailments / Sueños y otros achaques by Teresa Bevin

1st edition, ISBN 1-928589-13-8, (ISBN 13: 978-1-928589-13-6), $21.00

Winner of the 2001 Bronze Award for Translation—ForeWord Magazine's Book of the Year.
A wonderful array of short stories about the fantasy of life and tragedy but filled with humor and hope. "*Dreams and Other Ailments* will lift your spirits."— Lynne Greeley, The University of Vermont

The Gay Herman Melville Reader Edited by Ken Schellenberg

1st edition, ISBN 1-928589-19-7, (ISBN 13: 978-1-928589-19-8), $16.00

A superb selection of Melville's work. "Here in one anthology are the selections from which a serious argument can be made by both readers and scholars that a subtext exists that can be seen as homoerotic."— David Garrett Izzo, author of *Christopher Isherwood: His Era, His Gang, and the Legacy of the Truly Strong Man*

The Great Canopy by Paula Goldman

1ˢᵗ edition, ISBN 1-928589-31-6, (ISBN 13: 978-1-928589-31-0), $15.00

Winner of the 2004 Gival Press Poetry Award & Semi-Finalist for the 2006 Independent Publisher Book Award for Poetry.
"Under this canopy we experience the physicality of the body through Goldman's wonderfully muscular verse as well the analytics of a mind that tackles the meaning of Orpheus or the notion of desire."—Richard Jackson, author of *Half Lives, Heartwall*, and *Unauthorized Autobiography: New & Selected Poems*

The Last Day of Paradise by Kiki Denis

1ˢᵗ edition, ISBN 1-928589-32-4 (ISBN 13: 978-1-928589-32-7), $20.00

Winner of the 2005 Gival Press Novel Award.
"...Denis's debut is a slippery in-your-face accelerated rush of sex, hokum, and Greek family life. A little bit Eurydice, a little bit Chick-lit, with non-stop riffing on reality...."—Richard Peabody, editor of *Mondo Barbie*

Let Orpheus Take Your Hand by George Klawitter

1st edition, ISBN 1-928589-16-2, (ISBN 13: 978-1-928589-16-7), $15.00

Winner of the 2001 Gival Press Poetry Award.
A thought provoking work that mixes the spiritual with stealthy desire, with Orpheus leading us out of the pit. "These poems present deliciously sly metaphors of the erotic life that keep one reading on, and chuckling with pleasure."— Edward Field, author of *Stand Up, Friend, With Me*

Literatures of the African Diaspora by Yemi D. Ogunyemi

1st edition, ISBN 1-928589-22-7, (ISBN 13: 978-1-928589-22-8), $20.00

An important study of the influences in literatures of the world. "It, indeed, proves that African literatures are, without mincing words, a fountainhead of literary divergence."—Joshua 'Kunle Awosan, University of Massachusetts Dartmouth

Maximus in Catland by David Garrett Izzo
1st edition, ISBN 1-928589-34-0, (ISBN 13: 978-1-928589-34-1), $20.00
"... [an] examination of the idea of the Truly Strong Man—or, in this case, Cat—which is one who would give his own life for the sake of transpersonal good...This book is a treat—with a truly mystical message.—Toby Johnson, author of *Secret Matter*, winner of the Lambda Literary Award for Sci-Fi

Metamorphosis of the Serpent God by Robert L. Giron
1st edition, ISBN 1-928589-07-3, (ISBN 13: 978-1-928589-07-5), $12.00
"Robert Giron's biographical poetry embraces the past and the present, ethnic and sexual identity, themes both mythical and personal."— *The Midwest Book Review*

Middlebrow Annoyances: American Drama in the 21st Century by Myles Weber
1st edition, ISBN 1-928589-20-0, (ISBN 13: 978-1-928589-20-4), $20.00
"Weber's intelligence and integrity are unsurpassed by anyone writing about the American theatre today..."— John W. Crowley, The University of Alabama at Tuscaloosa

The Nature Sonnets by Jill Williams
1st edition, ISBN 1-928589-10-3, (ISBN 13: 978-1-928589-10-5), $8.95
An innovative collection of sonnets that speaks to the cycle of nature and life, crafted with wit and clarity. "Refreshing and pleasing."— Miles David Moore, author of *The Bears of Paris*

On the Altar of Greece by Donna J. Gelagotis Lee
1st edition, ISBN 1-928589-36-7, (ISBN 13: 978-1-928589-36-5), $15.00
Winner of the 2005 Gival Press Poetry Award.
"...the journey of our time at this altar offers us a striking, immense set of views of a world we thought we knew, and still, wonderfully, do know in much richer ways by the end."—Don Berger, author of *Quality Hill* and *The Cream-Filled Muse*

On the Tongue by Jeff Mann

1ª edition, ISBN 1-928589-35-9, (ISBN 13: 978-1-928589-35-8), $15.00

"...brilliantly pagan eroticism, at once tender, yet forceful and hard, like the hard-shelled seeds that spring from the fragilest of flowers. These poems are both, and in that breadth, nothing short of extraordinary..."—Trebor Healey, author of *Through It Came Bright Colors*

Poetic Voices Without Borders Edited by Robert L. Giron

1ª edition, ISBN 1-928589-30-8, (ISBN 13: 978-1-928589-30-3), $20.00

Winner of the 2006 Writers Notes Book Award—Notable for Art & Semi-Finalist for the 2006 Independent Publisher Book Award for Anthologies.
"...This book is edgy with a literary inclusiveness...Each voice is unique, yet together they create oneness even as they individually represent societal diversity."—Lucinda Farrokh, LareDOS: A Journal of the Borderlands

Prosody in England and Elsewhere: A Comparative Approach by Leonardo Malcovati

1st edition, ISBN 1-928589-26-X, (ISBN 13: 978-1-928589-26-6), $20.00

"To write about the structure of poetry for a non-specialist audience takes a brave author. To do so in a way that is readable, in fact enjoyable, without sacrificing scholarly standards takes an accomplished author."—Frank Anshen, State University of New York

Secret Memories / Recuerdos secretos by Carlos Rubio

1ª edition, ISBN 1-928589-27-8, (ISBN 13: 978-1-928589-27-3), $21.00

Finalist for the 2005 ForeWord Magazine's Book of Year Award for Translation.
"From the beginning, the reader feels pulled into the narrator's world and observes, along with him, a delicate, beautiful, and vulnerable universe as personal and intimate as a conversation between lovers."
—Hope Maxell Snyder, author of *Orange Wine*

The Smoke Week: Sept. 11-21, 2001 by Ellis Avery

1st edition, ISBN 1-928589-24-3, (ISBN 13: 978-1-928589-24-2), $15.00

Winner of the 2004 Writer's Notes Magazine Book Award— Notable for Culture & Winner of the Ohioana Library Walter Rumsey Marvin Award.
"Here is Witness. Here is Testimony."— Maxine Hong Kingston, author of *The Fifth Book of Peace*

Songs for the Spirit by Robert L. Giron

1st edition, ISBN 1-928589-08-1, (ISBN 13: 978-1-928589-08-2), $16.95

This humanist collection invokes a new vision, one that speaks to readers regardless of their spiritual inclination. "This is an extraordinary book."— John Shelby Spong, author of *Why Christianity Must Change or Die: A Bishop Speaks to Believers in Exile*

Sweet to Burn by Beverly Burch

1st edition, ISBN 1-928589-23-5, (ISBN 13: 978-1-928589-23-5), $15.00

Winner of the 2004 Lambda Literary Award for Lesbian Poetry & Winner of the 2003 Gival Press Poetry Award.
"Novelistic in scope, but packing the emotional intensity of lyric poetry..."— Eloise Klein Healy, author of *Passing*

Tickets to a Closing Play by Janet I. Buck

1st edition, ISBN 1-928589-25-1, (ISBN 13: 978-1-928589-25-9), $15.00

Winner of the 2002 Gival Press Poetry Award.
"...this rich and vibrant collection of poetry [is] not only serious and insightful, but a sheer delight to read."— Jane Butkin Roth, editor, *We Used to Be Wives: Divorce Unveiled Through Poetry*

Wrestling with Wood by Robert L. Giron

3rd edition, ISBN 1-928589-05-7, (ISBN 13: 978-1-928589-05-1), $5.95

A chapbook of impressionist moods and feelings of a long-term relationship which ended in a tragic death. "Nuggets of truth and beauty sprout within our souls."— Teresa Bevin, author of *Havana Split*

Books for Children

Barnyard Buddies I by Pamela Brown; illustrations by Annie H. Hutchins
1st edition, ISBN 1-928589-15-4, (ISBN 13: 978-1-928589-15-0), $16.00

Thirteen stories filled with a cast of creative creatures both engaging and educational. "These stories in this series are delightful. They are wise little fables, and I found them fabulous."
—Robert Morgan, author of *This Rock* and *Gap Creek*

Barnyard Buddies II by Pamela Brown; illustrations by Annie H. Hutchins
1st edition, ISBN 1-928589-21-9, (ISBN 13: 978-1-928589-21-1), $16.00

"Children's literature which emphasizes good character development is a welcome addition to educators' as well as parents' resources."
—Susan McCravy, elementary school teacher

Tina Springs into Summer / Tina se lanza al verano by Teresa Bevin; illustrations by Perfecto Rodriguez
1ᵉ edition, ISBN 1-928589-28-6, (ISBN 13: 978-1-928589-28-0), $21.00

Winner of the 2006 Writer's Notes Magazine Book Award—Notable for Young Adult Literature.
"This appealing book with its illustrations can serve as a wonderful learning tool for children in grades 3-6. Bevin clearly understands the thoughts, feelings, and typical behaviors of pre-teen youngsters from multi-cultural urban backgrounds...."
—Dr. Nancy Boyd Webb, Professor of Social Work, author and editor, *Play Therapy for Children in Crisis* and *Mass Trauma and Violence*

Inquiries: 703.351.0079
Books available
via Ingram, the Internet, and other outlets.
Or Write:
Gival Press, LLC
PO Box 3812
Arlington, VA 22203
Visit: *www.givalpress.com*